Coyote

Children Book of Fun Facts & Amazing Photos on Animals in Nature - A Wonderful Coyote Book for Kids aged 3-7

By

Ina Felix

Ina Felix

Copyright © 2015 by Ina Felix

All rights reserved. No part of this book may be used or reproduced in any manner whatsoever without the express written permission of the publisher except for the use of brief quotations in a book review. Image Credits: Royalty free images reproduced under license from various stock image repositories. Under a creative commons licenses.

I am a Coyote.

I am a mammal just like bears, cats, and cows.

I can be found in North America.

I live in deserts, grasslands, and scrublands.

I am related to dogs just like wolves, foxes, and jackals.

I live in a pack together with my fellow coyotes.

We hunt together to search for food.

I can rarely be seen alone as I am always with my fellows.

My favorite preys to hunt are sheep, birds, and cattle.

I also love to hunt for animals smaller than me to be my prey when I am hungry.

I love to eat meat just like any predators do.

My fellows and I protect our territory together from other predators.

I love to growl loudly in the night, especially when the moon is full.

I am a very good swimmer.

Some of us have a gray-colored fur, while others have red.

My babies are called pups.

We take care of our pups when they are little.

Pups are very playful and cute

Pups are trained to hunt just like the older coyotes.

I can become really big once I grow older.

Coyote

I hope you had fun learning about my family.

Thank you.

CPSIA information can be obtained
at www.ICGtesting.com
Printed in the USA
LVHW102137081220
673675LV00048B/971